POULTRY FARMING

HOW TO MARKET AND SELL POULTRY PRODUCTS

EFFECTIVE STRATEGIES, INVALUABLE TIPS AND TRICKS FOR PROFITABLE RETURNS

Disclaimer

This publication is designed to provide competent and reliable information regarding the subject matter. However, it is sold with the understanding that the author is not engaged in rendering legal or any other professional advice. The contents of this book are for information purposes only.

Although the author has made every effort to ensure the information herein was correct at the time of publication, the author does not assume, and hereby disclaim any liability to any party for any loss, damage, or disruption caused by errors or omissions; whether such errors or omissions result from negligence, accident, or any other cause.

Amazon, and the Amazon Logo are trademarks of Amazon.com Inc., or its affiliates.

Printed in The United States of America

If you are ready to learn today's effective strategies, invaluable tips and tricks for marketing and selling poultry products, this material is a goldmine!

Contents

WHY THIS BOOK IS A MUST-READ

Raising poultry birds such as chickens, quails, turkey, geese, guinea fowl, squabs, pigeon, partridge, emu, the tinamou's, pheasants e.t.c. but struggling with sales and marketing aspects of your operations? You are not alone!

The ultimate goal of every business-minded poultry farmer is to be able to maximize profits from the birds' products. However, it's sad to note that a good number of poultry farmers fail at this! They spend lots of time and resources raising the birds, only to get stuck at selling the precious products. And others who manage to sell do not make much from the sales. Interestingly, these failures aren't registered because of inadequate or shortage of demand for the birds' products in the markets, but simply because of relying on time-passed sales and marketing practices and strategies.

If you want to earn good profits from your birds' products, you must never neglect the sales and marketing aspect of your agribusiness. Truth is many poultry farmers get caught in the operations elements of raising the birds, too much that they give the sales and marketing aspects little regard. In the end, their profit margins suffer due to lower sales, and or due to selling the products at unfavorably lower prices.

This book is written for that poultry farmer struggling to find effective and profitable sales and marketing strategies. If you've been struggling with ideas and ways of marketing and selling poultry products such as meat, eggs, live birds, day old/week old birds, point of lay birds, old birds etc this is a perfect read.

LET'S START HERE

Sales is generally defined as an exchange of a given product / commodity / service/property with something of value such as money. Notably, when you read many books on the subject of sales, you'll be surprised to learn that it's widely defined as *"an act of selling something";* which is more of using a similar word to describe the same word.

On the other hand, I'm in love with how Dr. Philip Kotler defines marketing. He observes that *"Marketing is the science and art of exploring, creating, and delivering value to satisfy the needs of a target market at a profit. Marketing identifies unfulfilled needs and desires. It defines, measures and quantifies the size of the identified market and the profit potential".*

In a nutshell, selling entails persuading potential clients that your goods / products / services posses the relevant benefits / value they are after, while marketing is simply that process of identifying, expecting, predicting, and meeting the needs / requirements of clients, profitably.

Both sales and marketing are closely intertwined that many people find it hard to differentiate the two. In fact, in a number of small to medium-sized organizations / startups, employees end performing both sales and marketing assignments. No wonder in today's many organizations, you'll easily come a cross *'sales and marketing department'* - the two combined under one roof.

To any business venture engaged in selling products, poultry farming included, how the sales and marketing aspects are handled plays a vital role in determining the success or failure of that venture. Notably, the main objective of employing effective sales and marketing strategies is to help realize increase in revenue, which will resultantly witness the growth of that business in the long term.

Always remember, the approach must be strategic

Merriam-Webster defines strategy in numerous ways such as *"a careful plan or method for achieving a particular goal, usually over a long period of time", "a careful plan or method:*

a clever stratagem", ... "the skill of making or carrying out plans to achieve a goal", "a carefully developed plan or method for achieving a goal or the skill in developing and undertaking such a plan or method", ... Notably, strategy is widely utilized in the military circles as the *"the science and art of military command exercised to meet the enemy in combat under advantageous conditions".*

The word strategy is made of three key components; a goal, a plan, and action. An effective strategy would therefore entail proper identification of your goals, coming up with a right plan of actualizing those goals, and acting on that plan.

Strategic selling demands an effective and systematic approach, while being attentive to detail in the process. On the other hand, strategic marketing entails defining your clients, and clearly establishing why they buy what they buy? What sort of experience are they after? Significantly, it majors on establishing what clients what, produce/develop it, make it available to them conveniently, at the right price, and find ways of maintaining their addiction (loyalty) to that product/service.

Summarily

In poultry farming, you should strategically identify your goals; What you want to achieve, How big your operations should be, What sort of sales volume to expect over a given period of time, What new poultry breeds/ new farm equipments to bring in, etc. Plan in advance and commit to acting on that plan. Remember that planning without acting is simply a waste of time, while acting without any plan is a perfect route to that lonely town called failure.

The success of your poultry farming venture is literally tied to the success of your sales and marketing approaches. Therefore, you have no business venturing into poultry farming if you don't have solid sales and marketing strategies, especially if your aim is to derive profits from your venture.

Before delving deep, let me first take you through a critical area in sales and marketing, and that is trying to understand what influences consumers in general into buying the things they buy.

UNDERSTANDING WHAT INFLUENCES CONSUMERS INTO BUYING THE THINGS THEY BUY

If customers don't want it, they won't buy it. It's that simple

Did you know the ultimate goal of any produced product is for it to be easily accessed by the consumers? Remarkably, today's consumers are overwhelmed with a growing list of places where they can access the different goods and services they are in need of. But, have you ever wondered about what pushes people into buying the specific things they buy? There is an old age adage that *one man's meat is another man's poison.* What may interest a person in a given product or service may not necessarily interest the next person. World over, different people have different tastes and preferences for certain goods or services. Therefore, it's essential to understand what lures people into buying the specific things they buy.

Affordability

Having the purchasing power to acquire a given good or service plays a central role in influencing consumers into buying the things they do buy. You'll never easily find consumers buying things beyond their purchasing potential, with the exception of those taking bank credits to realize this.

Meeting a specific need

If say your car is out of gas, you would be headed to a gas station to re-fill it. Equally, if you have a toothache, you would be headed to a dentist for checkup. Still, anyone who wants to purchase a book would be headed to a bookshop or a bookstore - it wouldn't be easy finding someone looking for a book in a food restaurant; not unless that restaurant has a segment dealing with books. Most consumers end up buying what they are buying simply because of a specific need they intend to meet, save for isolated cases of impulse buying.

Good recommendations/reviews from past satisfied clients

Did you know positive product recommendations/reviews from past satisfied clients may bring in more sales and sales leads than a paid up media advertisement? That's how powerful a customer's feedback is! Notably, such positive recommendations/reviews have a unique way of influencing undecided clients into purchasing the products/services under focus. Interestingly, in a number of instances, such positive reviews have influenced a number of consumers into purchasing products or services that they have no urgent need of, to the advantage of the seller.

Credibility and Reliability

In a world littered with counterfeit products, many consumers usually embrace new products with lots of reservations. They want an assurance that their purchases are reliable enough to live their advertised potentials.

Occasionally, many would be tempted to make a few purchases to allow them first try out such new products, and will only re-surface to make future purchases should the products meet or exceed their expectations. But if their expectations aren't met, then they would have no urge of making any future purchases.

Pursuit of value for money

A growing number of people are cautious on how they are spending their hard earned money. On top of most shopping lists today, there is a demand for value of money utilized. However highly priced a product might appear, if its value matches with its price, then such a product would never desist being consumers' favorite.

Convenience

An anonymous notes that *we live in a microwave-like society.* Truth is, a growing number of consumers today have adopted purchasing of the ready-to-use kind of products. A typical example is the availability of ready-to-eat chicken meat from most supermarkets' shelves and food stores worldwide. Many consumers are on the look for such ready-to-use kind of products in pursuit of saving time, and possibly money.

The *freebie* influence

Who doesn't love gifts? Many consumers love freebies. However, they aren't necessarily looking for free goods or services, but are in pursuit of those products/services that may help them save a few coins. Notably, seasonal or occasional discounts on purchases or free samples (in case of new products) are usually very handy to many consumers. If given out strategically, it wouldn't be easy for consumers to forget such kind gestures, turning them into loyal clients for those products/services.

EFFECTIVE SALES AND MARKETING STRATEGIES FOR POULTRY PRODUCTS

Whether you are engaged in poultry farming on a small scale or on a large scale, in order to win the market share and stay relevant in your venture, you've got to utilize effective sales and marketing strategies. Here below are some of today's effective strategies you can consider putting into action.

Design a persuasive sales pitch (You'll use this everywhere)

Your sales pitch is an effective weapon in helping you convert potential clients into buyers. Did you know that almost 80% of people never read more than the first line of product reviews before making up their minds? There are a number of tricks you can utilize to help you draft an effective sales pitch, but my favorite one is: Grab attention, present problem/Solution, and then call to action. Summarily, grab the attention of your audience/potential clients - find a way of tapping into their emotions (showing them in just one line that they are definitely missing something(s) by not up taking up your products. In the problem/solution part, you can tell them how you understand their predicament of consuming 'the just normal poultry products' and that your solution is to offer them not only fresh and quality products, but equally affordably. In the call to action part, urge them to place their orders or to click on that buy button on your website (if you have one).

Employ services of sales and marketing personnel

If you want see an increase in sales, then simply employ services of sales and marketing personnel. One of the most cost-effective ways of engaging the sales and marketing people is by putting them on commission-based remuneration. Their earning is based on a percentage of sales they bring in. The more sales they bring in, the more they earn. And in equal measure, if they fail to bring in any sales over a given period of time then they simply don't deserve a pay.

Be present online / create a website

Design a good website, and use web design elements such as strong SEO's to help you attract online persons interested in poultry products. Having your own website gives you total control over all the vital aspects of that site. You'll have authority on deciding on what other plug-ins to add for great functionality and other extras. And most significant, the site will help you harness more buyers.

In designing the website, you'll need to have two vital sections: the home page, and products/sales page. Well, you can have as many sections as you would want, but these two should never miss. The home page, also commonly known as the landing page is that foremost page where your online visitors first *land* when they visit your website. It should be drafted with persuasive content, strong enough to turn the visitors into buyers. And the products page is where you list all those available products, and providing each listing with a buy button (buy link).

On the same website, you can embed social media apps such as facebook app or twitter app to enable you interact with clients. Equally important, you can create a form that enables any visitor to your site to sign up for any of your email newsletters or for notifications on available offers. Doing this will help you build not only a strong base of potential clients, but equally allow you reward your loyal clients by alerting them on availability of special offers.

Get some positive reviews embedded on your website

Having a great website is never enough! Did you know according to Everett Roger's revelation in diffusion of innovations theory, 'just about 14% of people are regarded as *early adopters*. The rest wants to know what others think of first'. The more positive reviews you'll have embedded on your site, the more proof you'll be able to provide to other potential buyers, possibly turning them into actual buyers in the end.

Engage in relationship marketing

Build a relationship with those clients you already have. Let them know that you not only take pride in them buying your products, but are equally sincerely interested in their day to day well being. Send them end-year wishes, birth day wishes, etc. Let them feel cared for and highly regarded. Resultantly, they will remain loyal to your products, ending up spending more money on those products. Additionally, they would bring in their close friends, colleagues, family, relatives (anyone within their cycle of influence).

Contact local hotels and restaurants

This is age old, yet still effective if correctly pulled. Get in touch with the managers, administrators, owners, and persons working in the local hotels and restaurants in pursuit of getting contracts to supply those facilities with the birds' products. Let them know that you can consistently meet their demands for the birds' products, while equally offering them favorable prices.

Initiate transactional marketing

Lunch promotional events like introducing coupons, discounts, special offers, and other incentive-filled sales events at the farm gate or at your retail/wholesale outlet. This is key to not only help you sell in high volume, but equally hands you an invaluable opportunity to get many new clients, and appreciate/reward the existing ones.

Utilize the word of mouth as often as you possibly can

This is an age old practice of relaying information from one person to the next via oral communication. It was and still is an effective way for customers to know of which specific products to purchase. Tell your existing customers to tell their friends, colleagues, family, relatives e.t.c. to purchase your poultry products. Word of mouth is an authentic and effective way to get many new clients; specifically those who have already heard the word of mouth testimony from other previously satisfied clients.

Use of freebies and free samples

Once in a while, you can offer your potential clients freebies and free samples as a way of 'snatching' them from the competition and to equally allow them have a feel of the top notch quality products you have. If utilized effectively, this strategy may bring you many potential buyers.

Partnership Marketing

Also regarded as affinity marketing, partnership marketing involves forming mutually beneficial alliances with other companies/organizations offering complimentary brands. As an example, you can link with a company manufacturing cooking oil; not to generate instant sales from such an arrangement, but to seek for new clients who are fond of utilizing that particular company's cooking oil. Even though the other company will generate more sales from offering your products as 'a thank you gift' to their clients, you on the other hand will have an opportunity to create awareness on your products and to find new clients. You can as well form an alliance with other companies dealing in poultry products in an effort to pull your resources together and sell your products cost-effectively.

Maximizing existing clients

To derive greater loyalty from the already existing clients, you should engage them as often as possible; seeking their views and offering them relevant discounts and special purchase prices. If handled effectively, you'll end up having these clients using word of mouth to help spread the 'good news' about your products to those within the circles.

Engage in business to business marketing

Find those small scale or even large scale businesses that can commit to taking up your products and using in their operations, or re-selling to others. If successful, you shall have created a consistent demand for your products over a good period of time.

Engage in business to consumer marketing

You can employ a business to consumer marketing campaign whose focus is to turn potential clients into buyers. Significantly, you can introduce things like special discounts, vouchers, discounts, free samples, freebies, unique displays, specially reduced prices on store front purchases etc, all geared towards luring your target clients into buying the products.

Utilize social media as often as you can

As already noted, create a facebook, twitter etc accounts to help you find and interact with customers online.

Create publicity for your products

This is broad! Publicity is generally all about raising awareness about your products, and more awareness will definitely yield more sales - as long as the publicity is correctly geared towards your target market. You can have a popular blogger blog about your products, get featured in a tv/radio show, get someone with great twitter/facebook followers to *post* about your products, frequent relevant poultry related exhibitions, or have adverts featured in the local dailies and newsletters with wider audience reach, etc.

Specifically, you can utilize the below to help you create publicity for the products:

- **Try viral marketing**

    Here, you can get your clients to share positive stories about your poultry products via social media platforms such as facebook, twitter, etc. If using Twitter, once a sizeable number of your clients decide to 'talk' about your products, it would take no time before it starts *trending*. And the moment it starts trending, then your products/brand shall have literally gone viral.

- **Also try mass marketing**

    Because many persons and organizations are engaged in poultry farming, the market is always awash with poultry products. To gain competitive edge, you must come up creative ways of driving a large number of clients to purchase your products. While engaging in mass marketing would require of you to spend much more on soliciting relevant data from the market, your efforts won't go in vain as you'll definitely be rewarded with a good insight as to where and how to execute your sales and marketing efforts. You'll have a perfect insight on who your potential clients are, where to find them, what their demands/requirements are, what message(s) to tell them, etc.... and all these would only be practically realized via getting honest feedback from your mass marketing efforts.

- **PR Marketing**

    One of the most effective marketing strategies is linking with the media to raise awareness on your products, and demonstrating how much value those not consuming your products are missing. Let your clients know that you are raising the right poultry breeds, under sanitary conditions, and that the birds are properly feed on well balanced and richly nutritious feeds. Always remember when it comes to food, people tend to place high regard to those nutritious products.

- **Initiate virtual marketing tours**

Well this is an out-box strategy that should help you create more awareness and hence more sales. There are several ways of implementing virtual marketing tours. If for example you reside in say area A, but wants to reach a targeted market in area B, you can have some popular person/people/relevant company in area B engage in marketing of your products (at an agreeable cost), without necessarily stepping in that area in person. After a given period of time (say three weeks or one month), you shift to area C, and have some popular person/people/relevant company in that area engage in marketing of your products. You then extend this to other areas. Other than using popular persons, you can have those products availed in popular food and food-related stores, with compelling adverts pinned in visible locations in those regions.

- **Online marketing**

Today's commerce has literally propagated to the internet, giving rise to online marketing. You can create strategic banners; static and pop ups, to help you 'trap' potential clients who visit certain websites or those who go online in search of poultry-related products.

- **Email marketing**

You can collect and organize email addresses of potential prospects, then send them relevant poultry -related emails. If correctly done, this is one effective way of connecting and engaging with clients, and helping you raise more awareness on your products.

- **Trade show and similar events**

Many customers throng events such as agricultural trade fairs, local farmers' agricultural exhibitions, to witness, learn, and even purchase some of the available products. Notably, trade shows offers a unique opportunity to meet new potential clients from all walks of life. And the bigger the trade fair, the more clients you should anticipate meeting.

You can organize to have a stall/space at such events, and bring along some of your carefully selected poultry products. Bring in those richly colored eggs, those big sized eggs, those healthy and elegant looking poultry birds etc. And of importance, give the clients an opportunity to sample out your products, and use that opportunity to show them how your products outsmart those of your competition.

- **Outbound Marketing / Direct marketing**

Develop a list of your potential customers and reach out to them via calls, emails, texts etc to let them know of your special offers (if any). You can as well outsource the outbound services to the organizations/freelancers offering such.

- **Promotional marketing**

This is a richly rewarding strategy geared towards influencing potential clients into buying given products or services. It should be packed with reward-related offers such as use of contests, free samples, special discounts, coupons.

Significantly, creating a contest and giving your potential clients a chance to participate in it doesn't only help you get more new clients, but also plays a great role in helping you create more awareness for your products.

- **Use of a newsletter**

If you have adequate resources, enough to put together a newsletter highlighting some of the positive aspects within your organization, then the use of a newsletter with a good clientele reach would help you harness a good number of new clients. You can write, or commission someone else to write and publish relevant content from your agribusiness (whose focus is to educate your potential clients about the benefits of your products).

- **Telemarketing**

Well, I guess you've already had an encounter with a telemarketer. While many people tend to view *the telemarketers' experience* as 'an uncomfortable one', an effective telemarketing plays a great role in helping many organizations world over to meet and even exceed their sales targets. In telemarketing, an individual solicits prospective customers into buying products, either over the telephone, web conferencing, Skype call, or through a face to face meeting (possibly arranged through a previous cold-call). Some organizations have gone ahead to program their telemarketing efforts by having recorded sales pitches playing over the phones via automatic dialing. Well, I wouldn't recommend you taking this route as it would possibly backfire (especially if you are starting out).

MANY PEOPLE ARE ALREADY ENGAGED IN SELLING OF POULTRY PRODUCTS, HOW DO YOU OUTSMART THEM?

Today, consumers are overwhelmed with options on where to purchase poultry products. Notably, the today's market place is littered with many sellers, offering similar poultry products at equally similar prices. Honestly, how many people do you know who are engaged in poultry farming as a hobby or as a business? Countless, I would readily guess. Therefore, you must think out of the box and come up with unique ideas in order to gain advantage over your competition.

But before taking you through some of the things you can do to outsmart your competition, let me first take you through what you already know; the four most common strategies utilized by over 60% of poultry farmers since time memorial to sell their birds' products.

a. **Farmer to trader:** In this approach, the farmer sells the products to traders in the local markets. Alternatively, the traders can pick up their purchases from the farm.

b. **Retail outlets:** Here, the farmer sells the products to food-related retail outlets such as restaurants, supermarkets, food stores etc.

c. **Supply to lead farmer:** Here, the poultry farmer supplies the products to lead farmers; those with huge contracts or growing demand.

d. **Supply to poultry related companies/groups:** In this arrangement, the farmer teams up with other interested poultry farmers and forms a group to exchange ideas, and to equally explore avenues of marketing and selling their products.

While these four approaches continue to help many poultry farmers world over to sell their products, it's essential to develop new strategies and approaches if you want to remain relevant and profitable in the already crowded poultry farming arena. And remember that the focus should be to position your products to enviably 'stand out' from the rest.

What then can you do to help you outsmart your competition and to have your products stand out from the rest? Take a look at the eighteen suggestions below:

1. Carry out regular market research

The only way to stay at par with latest consumer demands is by carrying out timely and regular market research. Doing so will allow you know how to improve the quality of your production, establish areas where there is insufficient supply or over supply, and unravel some things you can do to outdo your competition.

A good market research should help you understand and align your production. On your targeted audience, the research will help you understand the kind of poultry products your targeted market wants (whether it's more of eggs and less of meat, or more of meat and less of eggs...etc). Also, it should help you know the estimated population size of your targeted market, what their probable income potential is, what they like about your competitors' products - and what don't like about them, what they wish your competitors should have covered but so far haven't.......etc.

And on your competition, a good research should help you know how many poultry farmers are in that region, what kind of products they produce and what's their targeted market, their pricing, some of the challenges they are facing and how can overcome and outsmart such ...etc.

2. Have an online presence

This can never be overemphasized. Today, the continued uptake of education by a number of people world over has seen an increase in the number of people hanging around the internet. If your agribusiness isn't online, then you are definitely missing a lot. Having a website and utilizing social media accounts such as facebook, twitter etc is a rewarding way to not only promote your agribusiness, but to equally increase awareness of your birds' products.

You can regularly post those attractively packed fresh eggs or meat from your poultry farm on facebook or twitter, and your reward would be an increased uptake of those products by potential consumers. Being online isn't enough.

Find ways of enabling people to place their orders online, and equally establish increased ways of allowing the consumers to make their payments. When your business is online, even those people who would fail to place orders (probably due to lack of finances) would find it convenient referring other potential consumers to your site. And most significant, people would get an opportunity to correctly identify and purchase your products when availed in food stores, groceries or supermarket shelves.

3. Focus on quality production

Did you know the top things consumers are looking for in poultry products are good quality, freshness, size (properly sized eggs and lean meat), how clean the products are, and presentation – how the products are packaged. To enable you get products of high quality from the birds, you should exercise the below:

- **Invest in birds with proven good performance**

  If you want birds with the ability to lay a good number of eggs, then you should focus on raising those hybrid birds with proven potential to lay such number of eggs. Equally, if you wish for broilers with good body weight, ensure you get the right birds with such proven potential. The worst experience to subject yourself through is raising the wrong breed of poultry birds whilst expecting them to miraculously reward you with great products.

- **Feed the birds well**

  Properly fed birds grows stronger and mature fast, adopts the right body size, lays properly sized and nutritious eggs consistently over a good period of time. Failure to feed the birds appropriately will result into slow growth and inconsistent laying. In other words, when it comes to feeding poultry birds, the cardinal rule is that the quality of what they consume will always determine the quality of the birds' products.

- **Appropriate housing**

How the birds spend their time determines their production potential. Poultry birds detest crowded, noisy, pest infested, and rodent-prone environments. Ensure their accommodation is properly built, correctly located, properly spaced, clean, and has adequate and consistent feed and water supplies. Resultantly, they'll reward you with laying consistently over a long duration of time.

- **Handle the birds accordingly**

  Poultry birds generally detest rough handling. It scares them, resultantly making them less-productive. During normal bird management practices such as culling, de-beaking, vaccination, etc, handle the birds appropriately, always gently.

- **Exercise good egg production and management practices**

  The laying nests should be adequate, clean and rightly located. Immediately the eggs are laid, collect them on time and store in the right place appropriately (with pointed ends facing downwards - in a well ventilated room).

4. **Demonstrate the uniqueness of your products**

Show your clients that one thing, or even more, distinguishing you from other entities dealing in poultry products. Show them that one rare thing you are offering that they can't get elsewhere. Make it clear and measurable. And let that uniqueness be a reflection of your business mission and value.

One of my favorite unique value statements is by Domino's Pizza's - *You get fresh, hot pizza delivered to your door in 30 minutes or less — or it's free. L*ook at how unique and assuring that statement is! You can also take a look at the re-assuring value statement by M&M - *Melts in your mouth, not in your hand.* Clients want an assurance that your products are of indicated quality (of course high), and that by failing to uptake those products, they'll definitely be missing out on something.

5. Give them what others won't

Ever heard that customers often crave for what they can't have? In fact, they more often want things they aren't aware of! So why not give them both. Some customers may want to make an omelet, but don't know where to start. Package those eggs with instructions on how to make an omelet. You can also package those processed meat with instructions on how to make certain meat-related cuisines.

Simply find ways of giving them what your competition might be too busy to offer. If they purchase your product but finds out that its defective, what not encourage them to call your business directly, and have the product replaced at no, minimal cost, or even at an agreeable cost. Your uniqueness is an opportunity to get advantage over your competitors.

6. Deliver 'freshness', consistently

Guess you already know that 'freshness' is a top purchasing factor by consumers when it comes to food items. Just imagine the thought of a consumer purchasing an egg labeled *fresh,* only to encounter a spoilt/rotten egg when preparing a meal back at home! In all honesty, it would be a tall order trying to convince such a consumer that any eggs from that store or from that poultry company are fresh.

When it's labeled 'fresh', consumers expect it to be fresh, and should they encounter an otherwise experience, then they would simply avoid future purchases of that product.

7. Initiate home delivery services

Take advantage of those neighbors who are either too busy to make it to the grocery store to purchase the birds' products, or yearn for regular supply of fresh poultry products direct from the farm and offer them home delivery services.

You can expand your reach to cover those senior citizens, the sick, or any other person (nearby) who may be interested in home delivery services.

8. Introduce rewards

Introduce rewards such as free shipping/delivery, loyalty program etc to help lure potential clients your way, and to equally help you retain your existing clients.

9. Offer exclusive add-ons

Find creative ways of adding some exclusive add-ons. For say a crate of eggs bought, offer two to four eggs for free, or for a given number of live birds bought, offer a crate of eggs for free, or for a given specific number of purchases, offer free delivery etc. You can as well team up with other organizations and offer their products as exclusive add-ons to clients purchasing your poultry products in bulk. Find that one unique exclusive add-on that may lure your customers to want to come back for more purchases.

10. Create a strong support and training platform

Again, for those clients who do not know how to prepare/utilize poultry products, find a way of helping them before, and after making their purchases. Show them how to avoid common pitfalls in preparing certain poultry related dishes, or how to raise the birds accordingly (for those purchasing live birds), how to take care of the young birds, housing and feeding needs, how to handle the eggs etc. Doing all these shows how concerned you are about your clients' well being, helping you to develop and build strong relationships with them in the process. Resultantly, they'll reward you with their loyalty and even further referrals.

11. Pricing

Pricing is a very sensitive element when it comes to marketing and selling of poultry products. You definitely don't want your prices to be excessively high, or exceedingly low, but should be competitively and profitably set.

The keyword when it comes to pricing is 'affordability'. Once you've figured out your target market, avail to them the products at the right price and you'll definitely register a good uptake of the products, consistently.

Consider adjusting your prices favorably. Notably, although lowering prices is generally a good way to increase sales, it's largely unsustainable in the long run. Significantly, consider giving discounts on bulk purchases to help you realize more turnovers.

12. Engage in more promotional work

Have you ever bought something you had no prior knowledge of? Or have you ever bought anything you haven't heard of before? I guess seldom would be an ideal answer. And you are not alone! Most consumers buy what they already know, or have already heard of. Engaging in advertisements and promotions will help you create more awareness on your products/brand, thus allowing you increase sales.

Engage in more social media campaigns to enable you reach out to a good portion of your target market. As much as you don't necessarily need to re-invent the wheel when it comes to social media campaigns, you need to be creative, innovative and flexible. Truth is you aren't dealing in new, unique or original products, Poultry products have been in existence since time memorial.

13. Offer more 'convenience'

Find ways of availing the products conveniently to the consumers. Introduce the less' involvement' alternatives such as already-marinated meat, ready-to-eat meat balls that a mobile consumer can readily purchase and eat right away and etc... Equally, let the clients be aware of convenient pick up points for their purchases, or you can alternatively make deliveries to them.

If selling online, have your website designed to accommodate multiple languages (if possible), and Offer both return and money-back guarantees.

14. Offer more payment options

Give your clients a variety of options in making payments for their purchases. Other than cash and credit cards, you can introduce mobile money payment, or online-based money payment options such as pay pal and the likes.

15. Offer effective customer service/support

Let your clients know that should they encounter something worth making an inquiry about, they are free to get an appropriate response from your company, at any stipulated times. Always remember that if you can correctly sort out customer concerns in a timely manner, then they will reward you with their loyalty and other referrals.

16. Build trustworthy relationships with your clients

Engage them appropriately and accordingly. Have an open and faster way of resolving any of their issues, and regularly, communicate to them any relevant products news or available offers. Reward them appropriately (with genuine deals and specialized discounts). Seek for their honest reviews/feedbacks and be sincere about any of your shortcomings. Build trust, and be authentic in your dealings with them and most significant, be passionate about your products.

17. Create an abattoir

And why not have an abattoir where you can process, brand, package, and sell the products to consumers. Notably, when branding and packaging the products, ensure it's not only attractively done, but that it equally stands. Add some little bit of nutritional-related information on that packaging material since most consumers will be on the look for such.

18. Find ways of bypassing the notorious middlemen

Most middlemen in the poultry farming segment gets poultry products in bulk from farmers, then sell to others who in turn sell to consumers. They take advantage of farmers who have no proper timely knowledge on market prices, or those who simply want to sell their birds' products faster without giving due regard to prevailing market prices, or even considerable prices. While middlemen have helped many poultry farmers to consistently sell their products, depending on them yields dismal returns in comparison to what farmers would gain by selling directly to the consumers. One way of bypassing middlemen is by opting to sell both in wholesale and in retail quantities. You can set up a sales outlet in the local market, rent a store, or set up a store at the farm to help you realize this. Equally, you can team up with other farmers to form a co-operative kind of network to help you explore marketing opportunities.

LOOKING FOR MORE NEW CLIENTS? TRY THESE THREE APPROACHES

Well, there are several approaches you can pursue to help you get new clients, and I wouldn't love to limit your efforts to the only three covered herein. However, what I personally like about these three approaches is that they'll help you get loyal clients.

Networking

You can rely on your friends, family, relatives, past clients, a social event etc to get referrals of potential clients. The beauty of getting clients from networking is that a high percentage of those referrals have the potential to turn into long term loyal clients......and then you can get further referrals from the new ones, and the circle goes on, and on.

Advertising

While you'll have to spend a few dollars on advertisements, you'll be rewarded with good business leads and potential clients (should your advert correctly target the right audience). You can have your advertisements aired or placed in media platforms such as Tvs, radios, newspapers, magazines. Equally, you can have online-based advertisements running on social media platforms such as Facebook, Twitter, Linked In, Snapchat, etc.

Teaming-Up

You can team up with another non-competing company to leverage on available resources. For example, you might decide to offer other companies a good discount to enable them use your products as an incentive to clients who purchase their products. Equally, you can use other companies' products as gift items to clients who want to purchase your products.